Please renew/return

So that your telephone call
pleas

940.
531
JON

Re
Er
\

&

BC

# The Netherlands
## and
## Nazi Germany

*The Erasmus Lectures*

*1988*

# The Netherlands
# and
# Nazi Germany

*Louis de Jong*

Foreword by
*Simon Schama*

Harvard University Press
Cambridge, Massachusetts
London, England   1990

Copyright © 1990 by the President and Fellows of Harvard College
All rights reserved
Printed in the United States of America
10 9 8 7 6 5 4 3 2 1

This book is printed on acid-free paper, and its binding materials
have been chosen for strength and durability.

*Library of Congress Cataloging-in-Publication Data*
Jong, L. de (Louis), 1914–
    The Netherlands and Nazi Germany / Louis de Jong ;
foreword by Simon Schama.
        p. cm. —(The Erasmus lectures ; 1988)
    ISBN 0-674-60805-4 (alk. paper)
    1. World War, 1939–1945—Netherlands.    2. Holocaust, Jewish
(1939–1945)—Netherlands.    3. World War, 1939–1945—Underground movements—Netherlands.    4. Wilhelmina, Queen of the
Netherlands, 1880–1962.    5. Netherlands—History—German occupation, 1940–1945.
I. Title.    II. Series.
D802.N4J658    1990
940.53′18′09492—dc20
89-39692
CIP

# Contents

*Foreword*

# Louis de Jong and His History

*Simon Schama*

It has often been said that the bookshelf of every seventeenth-century Dutch home would contain two standard works: the Bible and the moralizing emblem books of "Father" Jacob Cats. On the shelves of the twentieth-century Dutch home one is almost as certain to meet with two other standard fixtures: the Dutch *Winkler Prins* Encyclopedia, and *The History of the Kingdom of the Netherlands in the Second World War* by Louis de Jong. They need to be stout shelves, for de Jong's monumental work of thirteen volumes contains twenty-six separate books—none of them exactly skimpy.

In its epic scale and narrative richness, de Jong's work seems to belong, despite its twentieth-century subject, to a much older, multivolumed, nineteenth-century historiographical tradition. Far from diluting its value, this connection to histories written before the rise of an institutionalized historical profession gives de Jong's writing its unmistakable quality of courage and integrity. His intellectual modus operandi has broken almost all the conventions within which academic history has customarily worked. He has taken narrative as his defining form during a period when analytical, problem-driven history has reigned supreme in university presses and periodicals. His particular style of narrative, dashingly written and vividly imagined, exemplifies the nineteenth-century confidence that storytelling and serious argument not only need not be separated but ought of necessity be linked if history is to be persuasive. De Jong has cared deeply about the forms of history precisely because he has, from the outset of his work, wanted to reach as wide a reading public as possible. In the same spirit, while academic history has insisted on dispassion and distance between the writer and his subject, de Jong has valued closeness and engagement. And while the academy has fought shy of anything resembling moral judgment in its writing—rejected again as the habit of nineteenth-century subjectivism—de Jong has been stirringly unapologetic about making precisely such judgments. To write of the Second World War and eschew such judgments strikes him as either preposterous or cowardly. "It seems to me almost impossible," he has said, "to describe that war as a struggle between, let us say, yellow and green."

Perhaps it is the magnificent temerity of his enterprise, as much as the brilliance and power with which it has been executed, that has lifted de Jong's work above the common run of historical writing in the Netherlands, so much of which in the last thirty years has been marked by an almost painful judiciousness. Sensing that they had been to some extent left to fend for themselves by the academic profession, the history-reading public in the Netherlands (a country famous for a staggeringly large book-buying public relative to its population), has embraced de Jong's work as a true chronicle, in the very best and most sophisticated sense, of the national experience. Each of his volumes has become an instant best-seller; together they account for many millions of copies. De Jong himself has become something like a national institution: a keeper of conscience, a witness of unimpeachable integrity and great moral force. His willingness, moreover, to see television documentary—and there is a tradition of superlative film documentary in the Netherlands—not as an enemy but an ally of the printed word has brought his history to an even more receptive and stimulated audience.

Predictably, none of this has happened without criticism. (In the Netherlands almost nothing does.) De Jong has been criticized for being too much a one-man show in writing a history that in other countries was entrusted to large committees. In fact of course where this has happened, such histories have invariably been dull, patchwork affairs, robbed of the vitality and coherence a single-author work can provide. Others have taken him to task for his devotion to narrative form, as if this somehow precluded sophisticated argument or set him apart from the debating conventions of academic history. But none of this has really convinced the vast majority of the Dutch public who have come to see de Jong's work as an indispensable and mighty thing, an act of conscience as much as an act of writing. Such a history has done what histories used to do: help whole cultures come to terms with their memory. Perhaps his many readers recognize in Louis de Jong a contemporary incarnation of the most courageous and creative traditions in Dutch historical writing—the tradition of Romein, Geyl, and Huizinga—impassioned, sometimes polemical; history written as a public act rather than worn as a scholarly habit.

From the beginning, Louis de Jong's history was necessarily connected with Dutch public life. As he explains in his third Erasmus lecture, he had spent much of the war working for the radio service of the Dutch government-in-exile in London, *Radio Oranje*. During that period he had already embarked on his vocation of gathering materials to document the history of the occupation of the Netherlands and the Dutch resistance. An early version of that work appeared—characteristically in four volumes—as *Je Maintiendrai*, the motto of the House of Orange, and a phrase which had come to be associated with the whole nation's fortitude in terrible times. When, immediately after the liberation, plans were being made to establish an

institute to document the Dutch experience of war and occupation, de Jong advised on its intended shape; when
plans came to fruition, he was appointed the first Director
of the Netherlands State Institute for War Documentation.
He remained in that post—as intellectual commander,
organizational manager, and literary pacemaker—for
thirty-four years. During that time he not only created an
archive of exhaustive completeness, he also brought its
resources actively to bear on issues, some of them painful,
that arose when unsettled business dating from wartime,
demanded ajudication.

De Jong also created the Institute's publications program, an enterprise that has produced remarkable work
on, for example, the destruction of the Dutch Jews and the
extraordinary 1941 strike against the Nazi regime in Amsterdam. But the incomparable tour de force of the Institute has been de Jong's own massive history, begun in
1955 and completed only in 1989 with a characteristically
provocative and critical volume on the tragic denouement
in Indonesia. Although no abridgment can do justice to
the documentary and intellectual breadth of the work, a
one-volume condensed version in English, prepared by
Dr. de Jong, would be an important addition to the litera-
ture of the Second World War. The chapters that follow are
not intended as that abridgment. They are instead a highly
personal meditation on many of the great themes that occupy the pages of de Jong's history, motifs that have

haunted his life and his writing and have made his work live, breathe, and endure. They are, I think, to be read more as a kind of testimony than a survey; nonetheless, they suggest many of the qualities of thought and feeling that inform his larger work.

Louis de Jong came to Harvard in the fall of 1988 to deliver the Erasmus lectures. Though in his seventies, he was full of a sparkling energy and enthusiasm that shamed jaded colleagues in their forties. Everything about the experience of living and teaching in New England that autumn delighted him, and he set about it with phenomenal gusto, whether charging up the stairs of Robinson Hall, dashing about the countryside in his rented car, or simply relishing the pleasures of living in the house of a former concertmaster of the Boston Symphony Orchestra. Above everything else, he threw himself into teaching a course on the Holocaust with a passion and dedication that astonished and flattered his students. Typical of his determination to have them confront the Holocaust as a human experience was his gathering a number of survivors from the Boston area to talk directly with the students about their experience, something they are unlikely ever to forget.

Those who heard de Jong deliver the first lecture of the Erasmus series recognized the unique quality of the moment, emotionally and morally charged, unapologetically subjective in its beginning recollections, almost unbearably poetic and poignant in its coda. It was a performance quite without artificial gesture or self-conscious academic mannerisms. At times more akin to confession than instruction, it was a lecture that probed deep below the skin of politeness conventionally assumed for such occasions. Eloquence hung in the dusty late afternoon air; it came to rest on responses that had been quickened and made open by the unmediated directness of de Jong's approach. It was the only lecture I can ever recollect where the measure of its power, sincerity, and depth of feeling commanded the audience to refrain from applause rather than break the skein of memory so tautly wound. No one who heard Louis de Jong that day could doubt that he or she had been in the presence of a great historian and, more important, a good man. This book echoes that resonating moment.

# The Netherlands
## and
## Nazi Germany

# The
# Holocaust

The Holocaust has been, and is, the central event in the life of every European Jew who is one of the survivors. One cannot speak about the Holocaust without being personal.

In May 1940, when the Netherlands were invaded by Nazi Germany, I was twenty-six. I was born in Amsterdam just before the outbreak of the First World War. At that time my parents were poor. Like so many other Amsterdam Jews, my father had been a diamond cutter. Slackness in the diamond industry forced him to become a peddler. The Jewish faith played no part in his life; he was a socialist and remained so when, later, he succeeded in building up a small business of his own, a dairy shop. He and my mother had but one aim in life: to ensure a better future for their children. So my twin brother and I were given every educational opportunity. Having finished high school, we attended Amsterdam University, he to study medicine, I to study history. After I graduated, early in 1938, a few weeks before the Austrian *Anschluss*, I joined the staff of a Dutch weekly which often warned people against the dangers of Nazi Germany.

I married in the autumn of 1939 and when, in May 1940, the German attack came, my wife, who was not Jewish, was expecting our first child. On the fifth day of the fighting, when it was clear that the Dutch army (my brother had been mobilized as an army doctor) would soon have to give up the struggle, we decided to try to escape to Britain by boat. So did tens of thousands of Dutchmen, among them many Jews; but nothing had been organized, it was difficult to approach the harbors, and there were hardly any ships. In getting to the coast my wife and I were accompanied by my parents, by my little sister who was nine, and by some of our best friends. Near the coast, where perhaps thirty thousand desperate people were milling about, my wife and I became separated from my relatives. Like most people, they returned home. We stayed. We found a boat. We were among the very few who succeeded in crossing the sea and reaching Britain.

In London I became a member of the staff of the broadcasting program of the Netherlands government in exile, *Radio Oranje*, Radio Orange. Until Pearl Harbor I managed to stay in touch, through the United States, with my parents and my brother and his wife. After that communication became more difficult; sometimes it was possible to exchange letters through neutral Portugal, sometimes there were only brief messages passed on by the International Red Cross. Early in 1943 I was given to understand that my brother and his wife had managed to hide their two children and were trying to escape. They never reached Britain. Having entered Switzerland, they were forced back into occupied France by the Swiss frontier guards. Some time later both were arrested near the Spanish frontier because there was a traitor in the escape group they had joined. My sister-in-law died in Auschwitz; my brother was evacuated from that camp in January 1945. After the war I was able to trace him to a small camp in central Germany, where he was still alive a few weeks before the end of the hostilities. Where, when, and how he died, I do not know. I never will.

In May 1943 in London the Polish socialist leader Szmul Zygielbojm, who had received news that his wife and children had been deported from the Warsaw ghetto, decided to commit suicide. Before doing so he wrote a letter to the press, pointing out that Polish Jewry, left on its own, had been well-nigh exterminated. In Britain there was but one paper, the *News Chronicle* (now defunct), which published his moving appeal. It made a deep impression on me. Zygielbojm's warning was confirmed shortly afterward when I read some reports on extermination camps that had been passed on by Gerhard Riegner, the representative of the World Jewish Congress in Geneva. That summer a Red Cross message, sent by my parents-in-law, informed me that my father, my mother, and my sister had been deported. I had but little hope that I would ever see them again, for I was one of the very few people in London who was convinced of the truth of what Riegner had reported. The Dutch prime minister, to name but one, was not. In November 1943 he asked me to accompany him for a weekend stay in a cottage outside London. I put the Riegner reports in my bag. On the first evening I said: "Sir, I want you to read this." He did. He looked at me in complete amazement. "De Jong," he said, "do you believe this to be true?" I said: "Yes." Did I convince him? I am not entirely sure.

Here we approach an aspect of the Holocaust which is of cardinal importance and which can never be sufficiently underlined: that the Holocaust, when it took place, was beyond the belief and the comprehension of almost all people living at the time, Jews included. Everyone knew that human history had been scarred by endless cruelties. But that thousands, nay millions, of human beings—men, women, and children, the old and the young, the healthy and the infirm—would be killed, finished off, mechanically, industrially so to speak, would be exterminated like vermin—that was a notion so alien to the human mind, an event so gruesome, so *new*, that the instinctive, indeed the natural, reaction of most people was: it can't be true.

As a professor of the Dutch university that bears the same name as the Chair that I have been honored to occupy—Erasmus University of Rotterdam—I have taught several courses on the Holocaust. Facing a younger generation, I have always started by saying: Forget about Auschwitz, forget everything you have heard, read, or watched on television about what happened in the extermination camps and the gas chambers, because, unless you do, you will be totally unable to follow and to understand the reactions both of the Jews and of the non-Jews.

With some exceptions, the only people who at that time fully realized what was going to happen to the Jews of the occupied Netherlands were the higher officials of the German administration, which was headed by a man who had played some part in the *Anschluss* of Austria, Arthur Seyss-Inquart. In 1940 his aim was to reduce the Jews to the same low status to which the German Jews had been reduced since 1933, that is, to deprive them of the businesses they had built up and, more important, to isolate them in Dutch society. The Holocaust having been decided upon in Berlin, in 1941, a second aim was superimposed upon the first: to have the Jews deported to the extermination camps in Eastern Europe. Trying to achieve both ends, the Germans, who were but few (though they were in command), needed help—administrative help, practical help, help from the Dutch civil service, help from the organs of the Dutch administration they closely controlled, help from the Jews themselves. They did not want any resistance; they insisted on compliance. First of all they intended to create a situation, akin to the one that had been realized in Germany, in which the non-Jewish majority would take but little notice of what happened to the Jews.

In this they failed. In the Netherlands there was not a single stage in the process of systematic persecution carried out by the occupier that was not accompanied by public protests and acts of resistance on the part of non-Jews.

In the autumn of 1940 the Germans demanded that no more Jews be admitted to the civil service; this was the thin end of the wedge. All organizations of university students protested, half of all university professors personally signed a letter of protest to Seyss-Inquart, and most Protestant churches (not yet the Catholic Church) joined this protest. When, in November 1940, all Jews were suddenly dismissed from the civil service, the students of two of our nine universities went on strike. A little later Dutch Nazis, who represented no more than 1½ percent of the population, were told to foment street riots against the Jews in all big cities. When, in the course of these riots, a Dutch Nazi was killed in Amsterdam, and a German police patrol was attacked by a small Jewish resistance group, the Germans decided to retaliate. On a Saturday afternoon and a Sunday morning in the Jewish center of Amsterdam over four hundred Jewish men and boys were brutally and viciously rounded up in full view of Jews and non-Jews alike. Indignation was so intense that, on February 25, 1941, virtually the entire working population of Amsterdam and a few other cities in the vicinity went on strike. The strike continued for two days, until the Germans broke it by force.

This strike, which, I believe, was the first and only antipogrom strike in human history, had an important effect on German policy. It made Seyss-Inquart and the other representatives of the Third Reich realize that they had to proceed with extreme caution. In doing so they made effective use of three important weapons: the weapon of fear, the weapon of dividing their opponents, and the weapon of deception.

The weapon of fear was directed against both Jews and non-Jews. The non-Jews were given to understand that every act of assistance to Jews was punishable. Vagueness being an important element of the entire German strategy, what sort of punishment would be imposed was never made clear, but virtually every non-Jew who tried to help Jews expected that, if found out, he would be sent to a German concentration camp. Indeed many were, but again many were not. With regard to the Jews, the Germans were more explicit. In the course of 1941 it transpired that the over four hundred Jewish men and boys who had been picked up in Amsterdam, as well as two more groups that had been arrested in May and in September of that same year—one totaling about three hundred, the other about two hundred people—had been sent to the concentration camp of Mauthausen in Austria where many of them had died. (In fact there is but one survivor of all three groups.) After that Jews in the Netherlands were convinced that to be sent to Mauthausen was tantamount to a death sentence, so in July 1942 the German announcement that Jews (they did not say: *all* Jews) would be sent to labor camps in Eastern Europe ("labor camps," mind you!) was accompanied by a statement of Himmler's personal representative in the Netherlands that every Jew who was detected in hiding, would be sent to Mauthausen. In fact, not a single one of those who were detected, was sent there; all were deported either to the concentration and extermination complex of Auschwitz-Birkenau or to the extermination camp of Sobibor in eastern Poland.

The second weapon, that of dividing their opponents, was also used against both Jews and non-Jews. The Germans never made it clear that they intended to deport *all* Jews; they realized that any such announcement might well unify the Jews and strengthen both Dutch resistance and the reluctance of the Dutch civil service to give any help to the program of persecution and deportation. Therefore, the Germans made many distinctions and many exceptions, thus creating a situation in which, German policy and German pressure being what it was, anyone who obtained permission for a certain group of Jews to be exempted from deportation felt that he had achieved a personal success of considerable importance. When the deportation of Jews was announced, the Catholic bishops and the leaders of all Protestant churches sent a moving letter of protest to Seyss-Inquart, informing him that they intended to have this letter read from all pulpits. The Protestant churches refrained from doing so, and in return they were given the assurance that all Jews who had embraced Protestantism would be exempted from deportation. The Catholic bishops had the letter read in public, with the result that a large group of Catholic Jews was immediately rounded up and deported to Auschwitz. Similarly the head of the Dutch civil service was told that he might draw up a list of Jews of outstanding importance in the fields of science and the arts; they too, a few hundred, would be able to remain in the Netherlands. Impulses to resist were broken by concessions of this nature—concessions which of course the Germans were determined to cancel the moment they thought fit.

Even more important, in my opinion, was the effect that the German policy of dividing their opponents had on the Jews themselves.

Early in 1941, shortly before the strike movement in Amsterdam, the Germans had ordered the principal leaders of the Jewish religious communities to set up a Jewish Council for Amsterdam, which eventually became the Jewish Council for the Netherlands.

The members of this Council, dominated by the Jewish bourgeoisie, realized from the start that they were going to act in a situation of extreme gravity. They were ordinary, law-abiding, well-to-do citizens, decently brought up, and they never realized what the Germans were up to. Having decided to act as a sort of separate Jewish administration, they adopted as their principle that they would never help in carrying out activities which, they stated, were "contrary to Jewish honor." The path of collaboration, however, is a most slippery one, and after some time a different principle came to dominate the proceedings and the activities of the Council. This was a most human but, given the circumstances, a most fatal principle: self-preservation. At that time about one hundred and forty thousand so-called full Jews were living in the Netherlands. (According to decrees based on the Nuremberg Laws, full Jews were Jews who had three or four Jewish grandparents or who, being half-Jewish, were married to full Jews.) These one hundred and forty thousand consisted of two main groups: Dutch Jews, and some twenty thousand immigrant Jews, nearly all of them refugees from Germany and Austria who before the war had been given shelter in the Netherlands. Like the father of Anne Frank, many of these refugees had been able to set up businesses of their own but in 1942, as in 1940, an important group was living in a camp at Westerbork, near the German frontier, that had been built by the prewar Dutch government. All members of the Jewish Council were Dutch Jews.

In March 1942 the Jewish Council was given to understand that the German Jews were to be deported to labor camps in Eastern Europe. The Council did not take any action; it even refrained from warning those representatives of the German Jews with whom it was in touch. The members of the Council evidently believed that the German Jews would be the only ones who would be sent out of the country. They were, therefore, deeply shocked when, after the introduction of the yellow star early in May and not a single German Jew having been deported, they were told in July that Dutch Jews too would be sent to the East. All of them? No, the Germans said, Jews whom the Council deemed important to carry out its many social activities would be allowed to remain in the Netherlands— at least for the time being. The Council fell into the trap. It drew up lists of some thirty-five thousand Jews. The lists were halved by the Germans and the Jewish Council accepted that only seventeen and a half thousand Jews would be exempted—all the others, one might say, were thrown to the wolves. In the middle of July deportations from the camp of Westerbork began. At that time, on the basis of a special registration of Jews that had been carried out early in 1941 by the Dutch civil service, the Germans decided which groups of Jews that had not been exempted were to be rounded up and sent to Westerbork. However, these groups all having disappeared, in May 1943 the Jewish Council was told that now it was their turn to indicate which Jews were to be deported: seven thousand in the first instance. They did. So it continued until, in September 1943, the members of the Jewish Council themselves were picked up and imprisoned in the Westerbork camp. They had performed their task.

I have failed to mention one factor which was of great importance: people's view of the progress of the war.

Why was it important? It was important because in the

summer of 1942 most people in occupied Europe firmly believed that very soon the Allied armies would land in Western Europe. At the end of May, when Vyacheslav Mikhailovich Molotov, Soviet Minister of Foreign Affairs, had visited Washington and London, an official announcement issued in London had said that the governments of Britain and the Soviet Union were in full agreement as to the desirability of setting up a so-called Second Front in Europe in 1942. To the Jewish Council this announcement meant that, as they saw it, only part of the Jews of the Netherlands would have been deported by the time the armies of the liberators arrived. They thought they would have saved the others through what they believed to be an effective policy of delay. But there were no Allied landings, at least not in Europe, and there was no delay. In drawing up their deportation plans the Germans assumed that, reckoning from July 1942, they would be able to deport all so-called full Jews within fourteen months. By and large they did. There was no resistance on the part of the Jewish Council.

Nor was there any resistance on the part of those German Jews who, closely controlled by the German SS, occupied all important positions in the Westerbork camp; their main function, following the instructions of the camp commander, an SS officer, was to draw up the lists of camp inmates who would have to board the trains that left for the so-called labor camps in the East. In the Westerbork camp too one principle dominated the activities of the tens of thousands of Jews, all of them helpless, who, having been transported by the Dutch State Railways, arrived in the camp only to be sent eastward after a delay of a few days or a few weeks or a longer period—the principle of self-preservation. No one knew what the conditions would be in the so-called labor camps; everyone realized that it would be best to stay in the Netherlands. However, it often happened that parents whose names had been put on a transport-list were joined by their children; this was true of Etty Hillesum, whose descriptions of life in the Westerbork camp are unsurpassed. There was not a single human impulse, whether noble or base, which the Germans did not make use of in implementing the Holocaust.

I now come to the third weapon the Germans used: deception. I have already indicated two forms of deception. One, the fact that people would be sent to labor camps which of course most of them readily believed, as Germany was already in dire need of every pair of hands that could help the German war effort. Two, the announcement that every Jew who was found in hiding, would be sent to Mauthausen. There was, however, a third form of deception, one which greatly influenced the policy of the Jewish Council. Upon arrival at Auschwitz-Birkenau, those Jews who were not selected for the gas chambers, but who were inscribed in the concentration-camp part of the complex, often were ordered to write postcards or letters to their families, informing them that they had arrived safely and that living and working conditions were tolerable. Many of these letters were not passed on, but several batches of them did arrive in Amsterdam; the first batch, fifty-two postcards, arrived four weeks after the first deportees had left Westerbork. I will quote one letter, taken from a batch that arrived in the middle of December 1942. This particular letter was despatched from the notorious camp of Auschwitz III, the I.G. Farben works at Monowitz, where a total of thirty-five thousand prisoners were set to work of whom no less than twenty-five thousand perished. "I have now been here four weeks," the letter said, "and I am well. I am in good health. Work is not particularly heavy. We start at seven in the morning and we work till four in the afternoon. Food is good: at noon we have a warm meal and in the evening we get bread with butter, sausages, cheese, or marmelade. We have central heating here and we sleep under two covers. We have magnificent showers with warm and cold water."

Other letters were less reassuring. In fact in January 1943 staff members of the Jewish Council, having scrutinized a new batch, all sent by men, found it disquieting that there was not a word in these letters referring to the wives, the children, and the older people who had accompanied these men when they left Westerbork. All in all, until September 1943 some fifteen hundred postcards and letters were passed on to the Jewish Council—a few of them with clear and courageous warnings, one ending with a Dutch-Jewish expression equal to "tell it to the Marines!"

All these warnings were disregarded.

Similarly, the fact that the Germans allowed, and even encouraged, Jews remaining in the Netherlands to send letters to relatives who had been deported fortified the belief of members of the Jewish Council and many others that the people to whom those letters were addressed were still alive. Tens of thousands of such letters were handed to the Germans. Of course not a single one was ever delivered.

Now I want to give you a few figures as to the fate of the deportees.

In 1943 and 1944 some groups of Jews were privileged to be transported either to the exchange-camp of Bergen-Belsen or to the so-called preferential ghetto of Theresienstadt. Nearly four thousand from the Netherlands were sent to Bergen-Belsen; there were two thousand survivors. Nearly five thousand were sent to Theresienstadt, including the Protestant Jews, those who had been listed by the head of the Dutch civil service, and the principal members of the Jewish Council; again two thousand survived. Sixty thousand Jews were deported to Auschwitz; there were nine hundred and seventy-two survivors. Thirty-four thousand Jews were deported to Sobibor (including my parents, my sister, and most members of my family); of the nineteen survivors, however, seventeen were in Sobibor only a few hours before being sent to a different camp. Of the thirty-four thousand others, two (both young women who took part in the heroic Sobibor uprising, one of whom now lives in Connecticut) were able to return. Two out of thirty-four thousand, no more.

All in all, and including some groups that were deported to camps other than those I have mentioned, more than one hundred thousand Jews from the Netherlands were killed by the persecutors.

I have not yet finished.

There are two obvious questions which I shall try to answer. One, to what extent did the Jews of the Netherlands accept the authority of the Jewish Council? Two, to what extent did they resist?

As to the first question, there is no doubt that most Jews never accepted the authority of the Jewish Council. Particularly in 1942 and 1943 the Council was seen by them—and, in my opinion, rightly so—as an organ that was wholly subservient to the Germans. If they conformed to the announcements the Council made, they did so not because it claimed to represent them, but because it was backed by the overwhelming power of the German occupier: by his army, by his police, by his secret police, by his Dutch informers. Nevertheless, there were several instances when many of the Jews of the Netherlands refused to conform what the Council decreed. For all forms of social and economic activity one needed the Council's assistance, which, however, was only given after one had paid a sort of Jewish special tax, a very small sum. One-third of all Jews never paid a cent. Next, early in 1942 in Amsterdam twenty-six hundred Jews were ordered by the Council to report for work in Dutch labor camps; only nine hundred did so. Next, when the deportations started, Jews were strongly urged by the Council to be present on time at the railway station in order to be transported to Wester-bork. About 50 percent simply refused to show up. Finally, in May 1943, as I have said, seven thousand Jews in Amsterdam lost their exemption; they too were ordered to be present on time for their departure. Only seven hundred turned up.

Refusals to bow to the authority of the Council were by themselves, as I see it, simple acts of resistance. There were such acts.

First of all I would like to underscore the fact that the percentage of Jews who joined the general Dutch resistance movement was significantly higher than that of non-Jews. There is not a single form of general Dutch resistance activity in which Jews did not take a prominent part.

Second, many thousands of Jews tried to escape from the occupied Netherlands, as my brother and his wife did. Each of them had to face the gravest perils. The Netherlands were more isolated than any other country in Western Europe. If you tried to escape from France, there was but one frontier you had to cross. From Belgium two. From the Netherlands three. Exactly how many were captured trying to escape we will never know, but it is a reliable estimate that some fourteen hundred Jews from the Netherlands managed to enter Switzerland before the Swiss closed the frontier to Jewish refugees, that perhaps two hundred managed to hide in Belgium and France, and that thirteen hundred were able to reach Spain and Portugal. Most of those who succeeded in escaping were magnificently assisted by resistance organizations in the Netherlands, in Belgium, and in France.

Next, there is the vast group of Jews who decided to hide in the Netherlands. I am sure that everyone who has read the diary of Anne Frank has a clear picture of the perseverance and the courage that were needed not only to go into hiding but to stay in hiding, week after week, month after month. Mind you, the case of the Frank family was a rather unusual one. Very few Jews had a hiding place of their own like the one Anne's father managed to construct; most were hidden in the homes of non-Jews. However, all who went into hiding faced the same difficulties. If possible, they had to obtain false identity papers, they had to obtain food coupons, and many of them were in need of money. My estimate is that out of the one hundred and forty thousand so-called full Jews who were liable to be deported, about twenty-five thousand went into hiding. We know that about one-third of them, eight-thousand, were either detected or betrayed, as was the Frank family, and deported.

How many non-Jewish families had the courage to open their homes, and often their hearts too, to their persecuted cocitizens? We do not know exactly. In some places only one Jew was given shelter, in others ten or more. In some places Jews stayed only for a brief period, in others for nearly three full years, each of which seemed endless. One Jewish child was given shelter in twenty-four different hiding places. My estimate is that the number of homes where Jews were kept hidden, may well have been twenty-five thousand, and my further estimate is that there were at least two to three thousand resistance workers whose main or exclusive activity consisted of finding hiding places, papers, food coupons, and money for Jews in hiding and of solving their endless and often nerve-racking practical and personal problems.

Some of these Righteous Gentiles, as they are called by the State of Israel, have been honored by the Yad Vashem Institute in Jerusalem. Most of them did not receive nor did they claim any recognition. Their conviction was that they had merely done their duty as human beings, and, in the contacts I have had with members of this group, it has struck me that many of them felt they had not done enough.

Can one draw up a balance of what I have tried to explain? It is difficult, but I would like to make a few observations.

There is, at first sight, a strange contradiction between two facts: that proportionally more Jews were deported from the Netherlands than from any other country of Western Europe, but that there was not a country in Europe, and perhaps in the whole Christian world, where there was less anti-Semitism than in the Netherlands. Some anti-Semitism there was, but it was mild. Elsewhere Jews had been victims of pogroms or had been herded into ghettos or had to suffer constant indignities or had to live in countries where, from time to time, major parts of the population allowed themselves to be swept along on a strong current of anti-Semitism. Think of what happened in the Ukraine and in other parts of the Pale of Settlement, in Poland and Rumania, in Germany and Austria, in France at the time of the Dreyfus Affair. I would not say that life in the Netherlands was easy for Jews, most of whom were rather poor, but it was certainly less difficult than elsewhere. They felt at home. They felt more or less safe and, from a desire to ensure their safety, they were, generally speaking, more law-abiding than Jews elsewhere, more obedient, less wary, less suspicious, less aggressive. There is, therefore, no contradiction between the two facts I have mentioned. On the contrary: one may say that, faced with the Holocaust, which was as murderous as it was relentless, the Jews of the Netherlands, having found shelter in a country that was rightly famous for its tolerance, were the victims of their own past.

Nowhere was the struggle for life more ferocious, more desperate, than in the chaos, filth, and crushing misery of the concentration camps. Jews from the Netherlands found it more difficult than other Jews to fight for a crust of bread or a spoonful of soup or a less bone-breaking job. Their decency was their undoing. In the period from July 1942 to February 1943, from all transports from Westerbork camp, on the average one hundred and sixty male deportees were not sent immediately to the gas chambers but were shipped either to Auschwitz I or to Auschwitz II, Birkenau. In Birkenau alone there were nights, immediately following their arrival in the camp, when thirty of these one hundred and sixty male deportees committed suicide, mostly by throwing themselves on the barbed wire of the electrified fence. Figures for the cases of suicide among Dutch Jews are significantly higher than similar figures for Jews from other countries.

Of Sobibor there is nothing left but a heap of ashes. As to Auschwitz, more than twenty years ago I went there. Auschwitz I, the original camp, was, I felt, too much of a contrast to what it had been at the time of the Holocaust: too well-preserved, too well-ordered, too placid. Everything I saw—the empty but tidy barracks, the magnificent trees, the museum even—interposed itself, the reality of the 1960s covering so to speak the reality of the 1940s.

Auschwitz II, Birkenau, however, was nearly bare. A gatehouse, a few drab barracks, a railway track, a ramp, and, where the chimneys of the gas chambers not flattened by Allied or Russian bombs had risen into an indifferent sky, a few heaps of stones. Here free rein was given to that human faculty essential for any historian: his creative but controlled imagination. Creative because he has to combine everything he is and everything he knows in order to recreate the past, controlled because he has to stay within the sober bounds of what really happened. Standing there all alone, I had an overwhelming feeling of being right in the middle of a vanished world of suffering, infinitely distant from my own country. Silence was absolute. There was not a bird in the sky. There was a faint smell of a foul morass. There was an atmosphere of indescribable danger. I was on the edge of the universe, on the edge of life itself, facing, as so many had done, extinction.

"Men," the French philosopher Larouchefoucauld has said, "cannot look directly at either the sun or death" (*le soleil ni la mort se peuvent regarder fixement*). There is no saying that is more apposite to the Holocaust. The Jews of Europe were facing death. No one can blame them for not fully recognizing that overwhelming threat. I say not *fully*, because I believe the facts show that many of them were driven by urges that can only be explained by their awareness, however dim, however vague, that life itself was at stake.

Most of them had no chance.

What had been built up in the heart of Europe was a tremendous machinery of destruction, powered by the energy of an evil doctrine, making use of the cogs and wheels of every form of official organization, German and non-German, even Jewish, grinding millions of helpless and innocent people to dust.

To posterity the Holocaust points out a warning which mankind will ignore only at its peril.

It has left us, the survivors, with wounds that will never heal and with tears that will never dry up, but also with the unshakable determination faithfully and soberly to record what happened, to proclaim and defend what we know to be the truth, to care for the victims, to honor all who helped, to protect the embattled state of Israel, and to see to it that, however late, justice is meted out to everyone who took part in that unspeakable crime.

# The Anti-Nazi
# Resistance

Resistance appears to be a subject full of romance. The press, books, broadcasting, and, perhaps most of all, television have presented us time and again with stories of stirring adventures, incredible suffering, and heroic triumphs. We have admired time and again men and women making up their mind to join a resistance group, to face persecution by the German secret police, the Gestapo, to brave the dangers of being captured, tortured, sent to prisons or concentration camps, or being shot. The secret agent in particular has been a subject of endless fascination. We have seen him being trained, parachuted into an occupied country, starting on his dangerous mission, hiding with patriots, sending and receiving strings of coded messages, penetrating enemy strongholds, gathering military information, preparing and carrying out daring acts of sabotage, destroying the German war effort.

Facing Germany, and facing it alone, Great Britain in the fateful summer of 1940 was in possession of but one secret service, Military Intelligence, bent on collecting information on the strength and the location of the armed forces of the Third Reich. It was Winston Churchill who decided to set up a second secret service, the Special Operations Executive, or SOE; its task would be to undermine German morale, to foster widespread sabotage, and to organize underground armies. The order Churchill gave to the minister concerned consisted of only three words— "Set Europe ablaze"—and the picture given by the press, books, broadcasting, and television has often given the overall impression that during the years of Nazi oppression Europe was a continent seething with the fires, small and great, of resistance, and even rebellion.

Is that picture totally wrong? Is it based purely on fiction? Is it but a product of communication media catering to the taste of a tired audience? Certainly not. But it is unbalanced. The most famous of this century's Dutch historians, Johan Huizinga, once wrote that history, like good sherry, should be dry. What we have been served too often in texts or programs dealing with the resistance movements must be called champagne. I love champagne, but not in carrying out my profession.

I intend to present a more balanced, a more sober survey and analysis of anti-Nazi resistance in the Netherlands during the five years of German occupation.

First let me give you a few basic facts. The Netherlands, which were occupied by Nazi Germany in May 1940 after a brief campaign, were a small but densely populated country. They still are. In 1940 some nine million people lived in a total area of 33,000 square kilometers—the country is one and a half times the size of Massachusetts. Virtually all the land was either built on or under cultivation; woods and similar areas occupied only 7 percent. Excellent roads linked even the smallest villages and hamlets; there was nationwide railway and bus transportation and a telephone and telegraph system.

Most of the country was perfectly flat. An elevation of twenty or thirty feet was called a hill. The highest one just topped one thousand feet; it, like a score of others that were lower, was proudly called a mountain. There was no space nor were there any natural features that would have enabled the setting up of a *maquis*, an area where men and women planning to offer armed resistance to the occupier would be able to create an administrative or even a governmental system of their own, however primitive. This was possible in the occupied parts of the Soviet Union, in Poland, in Czechoslovakia, in Greece, in Yugoslavia, in Italy, and in France—but not in the Netherlands. Perhaps no other country could be held in a state of subjection by so few troops, provided these were well armed and could, in case of need, be swiftly moved from one place to another. In the Netherlands, garrisoned by two or three German infantry divisions and a few regiments of police, this would never take more than a few hours. There were but two German-occupied countries where geographical circumstances were not essentially different: Denmark and Belgium.

The Netherlands, however, were more isolated. The coast of the North Sea, which separates the Netherlands from England, was closely watched by the Germans; no more than some hundred and fifty Dutchmen succeeded in escaping to Britain in small boats or canoes. Compare that to German-occupied Norway: no fewer than eighty thousand Norwegians managed to slip into neutral Sweden.

Moreover, the Netherlands were situated on the direct route between the airfields of the British Royal Air Force and, later on, the American Eighth Air Force and the Ruhr Basin, where a sizable part of German industry was located. Concentrations of German antiaircraft artillery were particularly dense, and many squadrons of German fighters were stationed on Dutch airfields. This hampered the dropping of secret agents and of supplies for the resistance groups. After some time British Military Intelligence and SOE were able to conduct a regular courier service to occupied France, making use of aircraft which landed on secret airfields. In the Netherlands this was out of the question. By and large therefore Dutch resistance was a lonely affair. For the most part people had to act on their own.

What did they achieve? Dutch resistance, as is indicated by the word itself, was a reaction to German policy, so in order to determine what Dutch resistance did or did not achieve, it is necessary to indicate first what the Germans intended to achieve.

The Germans had set themselves four goals. The first was to transform the Netherlands into a national socialist state, which in one form or another, Germany having won the war, would be amalgamated into Nazi Germany or into *das Grossgermanische Reich*, as many Germans called it, particularly those who had joined the increasingly powerful SS. The second aim of the Germans was to exploit fully the Dutch economic potential, including the Dutch labor force. Their third aim was to purge the Netherlands of Jews. Their fourth aim was to prevent all aid to Germany's enemies, whether by espionage, by sabotage, or by guerrilla activity. Many people today equate resistance with activities aimed at thwarting that fourth German aim— spies, saboteurs, and guerrilla fighters being seen as the true representatives of the resistance movement. This view, in my opinion, is far too narrow. Every act that opposed any of those four German goals was an act of resistance; those activities directed against the fourth German aim might best be called underground activities. The underground groups or the underground movement were only part of much wider manifestations of resistance against the foreign occupier. This becomes clear the moment we ask to what extent the Germans were able to achieve not only their fourth aim, but also their first, second, and third.

In their first aim, to transform the Netherlands into a national socialist state, they failed completely. The Dutch Nazi movement never won the support of more than 1½ percent of the Dutch population. Moreover, as early as the summer of 1940, even before the Battle of Britain had been won by the British Royal Air Force, the majority of the population had but one conviction—that Germany would lose the war—and but one desire—that Dutch independence should be restored. This attitude was made clear by countless small acts. Despite German bans, people tuned in to British, some also to American broadcasting stations, and they performed all sorts of small acts (they might be called acts of "symbolic resistance") that showed their true feelings. Stamps, for instance, were affixed to the left-hand corner of envelopes because, people said, the right-hand corner belonged only to stamps with the image of Queen Wilhelmina, who was living in exile in London. I give you another example. There is no greeting simpler than "hallo," but from the summer of 1940 on, the letters of this word were widely regarded as the abbreviation of the words of a short sentence: *Hang alle landverraders op*, which means "Hang all traitors."

This general anti-Nazi attitude manifested itself in the three famous Dutch mass strikes which occurred during the occupation. First, in February 1941, the strike of the people of the city of Amsterdam to protest the persecution of their Jewish cocitizens. Second, a virtually nationwide strike in the spring of 1943, when the Germans announced that all members of the Dutch armed forces, whom they had released from captivity after their victory in May 1940, would have to report to be sent to prisoner-of-war camps in Germany. Third, the strike of the Dutch railwaymen, ordered on September 17, 1944—the day the Allied Airborne Army landed near the big rivers (the

Lower Rhine), cutting off a small part of the country—by the Dutch Government in a radio broadcast in London, and which, Montgomery's attempt to cross the big rivers having failed, had to be continued for nearly eight months. Here we have three important manifestations of a spirit of resistance animating hundreds of thousands of people.

This general anti-German attitude was of basic importance. It was not only the foundation of all kinds of underground activity but also of all kinds of resistance to German attempts at Nazification. There was resistance on the part of the leaders of the country's six most important prewar political parties, who, in July 1940, having drawn up a common program, refused to have it published because the Germans had crossed out all references to the Royal House of Orange and to independence. There was resistance on the part of the churches, which time and again voiced their indignation in courageous pastoral letters, most of which were read from all pulpits. There was resistance on the part of the members of the trade unions and of the organizations of employers, on the part of the farmers, of many artists, particularly writers and sculptors, and of virtually all members of the medical profession, when they were told that the organizations they had built up would be superseded by new ones, led by Dutch national socialists—new organizations that were replicas of those of the Third Reich. In April 1943, when university students were ordered to sign a declaration of loyalty toward the occupying authorities, 85 percent refused to do so. Arriving in the Netherlands in May 1940, the Austrian Arthur Seyss-Inquart had high hopes that as Hitler's *Reichskommissar,* or Reich Commissioner, he would be able to prepare the Netherlands for their eventual absorption into *das Grossgermanische Reich.* Before a year had passed he must have realized that these hopes had to be deferred if not abandoned.

Seyss-Inquart was more successful in achieving his second aim: to exploit fully the Dutch economic potential, including the Dutch labor force. The Netherlands were (and are) a trading nation, Germany being their most important trading partner. More than that, once they had been occupied, the British blockade made them wholly dependent on Germany for the import of raw materials. These the Germans were willing to supply, provided Dutch industry turned out the products the German war effort needed, including weapons. In the summer of 1940 there was some hesitation whether or not to comply with this German demand, but the situation itself and German threats convinced the Dutch German-supervised administration and the Dutch industrialists that, if they intended to save their industries and to keep their workers employed, they had no choice but to accede to the German wishes. So they did. Broadly speaking, half of Dutch industry worked exclusively for the German war effort, with more than half of the German orders pertaining to military supplies. In 1943 (the only year for which detailed figures are available) 2 to 3 percent of all the weapons the German armed forces acquired were produced in the Netherlands; this, however, included 8 percent of all radio sets and 14 percent of all shipping. German control being very strict, cases of sabotage (although they did occur) were few, and it is noteworthy that the Germans were satisfied with the speed of Dutch deliveries. In this respect Dutch industry was quicker than the Belgian or French. At the end of 1943 French industry had delivered 70 percent of all orders placed by the Germans since the early summer of 1940, Belgian industry 76 percent, and Dutch industry 84 percent. In the first half of 1944, however, there was more resistance on the part of the Dutch industrialists, and in the period after September 1944 their contribution to the German war effort fell off. Most of the country south of the big rivers had been liberated, including the area where the only coal mines were situated. North of the big rivers, where there were hardly any energy supplies, such trains as the Germans managed to keep running (with German personnel) were used to transport to Germany a large part of all Dutch industrial machines.

I pointed out that the Dutch industrialists not only intended to save their industries but also to keep their workers employed; these, if no work was available in the

Netherlands, might well be sent to Germany. In the spring of 1944 total industrial production had been halved, compared to the preinvasion figures, but the number of industrial workers had remained more or less the same. In this respect, therefore, Dutch industrialists had been successful. Nevertheless, by that time many workers were employed in Germany. In 1940 and 1941 a number of volunteers went there, but the Dutch administration had also forced many unemployed to accept work in Germany, saying that if they refused to go, they would lose all unemployment benefits. Of those who went, about one-third returned almost immediately to the Netherlands on their own. Later this pattern was repeated. Workers either left their places of employment in Germany or, having been permitted to spend a brief holiday with their families, refused to return to Germany. Some, when called up for the first time to go to the enemy country, got in touch with underground groups which helped them to go into hiding. Altogether about half a million Dutch workers were forced to work in Germany, but at the end of the war the number of those who, contrary to orders received, had managed to stay in the Netherlands, where they had gone into hiding, was more than three hundred thousand.

My conclusion is that by and large Seyss-Inquart did achieve some measure of success with regard to the second aim of German policy. The wartime economy of the occupied Netherlands was indeed integrated into the wartime economy of Nazi Germany, and its contribution, though certainly not a maximum one, was not inconsiderable.

There may seem to be a strange contrast between my first two conclusions: the people of the Netherlands said "no" to national socialism, but their contribution to the German war effort was not inconsiderable. Is this difficult to understand? I do not think so. People may hate a foreign occupier, but if there is no opportunity to withdraw from the areas where he is in command (and for geographical reasons this opportunity did not exist in the Netherlands), the economy of an occupied nation will inevitably be forced to become part of the economy of the occupier. In this respect there is nothing new in what happened in the Second World War. In fact there are many areas in the present-day world where the same conditions prevail. First of all, people have to eat and, as Bertholt Brecht put it in the *Beggar's Opera, "Erst kommt das Fressen, dann kommt die Moral,"* "First comes the grub, and then morality."

I now come to the third aim the Germans had set themselves: to purge the Netherlands of Jews. Here again, alas, they achieved a considerable measure of success. The German intention was to deport and kill all so-called full Jews, totaling one hundred and forty thousand. Of these about ten thousand were partners in what were called mixed marriages; most of these Jews, married to a non-Jewish husband or a non-Jewish wife, were not to be deported for the time being, this being in accordance with the practice followed in Germany itself. I do not think there is any reason to doubt that, had Germany won the war, the Jewish partners in mixed marriages would have suffered the same fate as all other full Jews, and probably they would have been followed by all so-called half- and quarter-Jews, that is: Jews with either two Jewish grandparents or only one. However that may be, of the one hundred and thirty thousand remaining full Jews, the Germans succeeded in deporting no fewer than one hundred and seven thousand, slightly more than 82 percent.

How was this possible? I give you six reasons.

First, virtually no one realized the fate that was in store for all those who were deported. Second, German deception was both cunning and effective. Third, compared to Jews in other countries the Jews in the Netherlands were less vigilant. Fourth, they received virtually no help whatever from the Dutch authorities in the Netherlands. Fifth, deportations started nearly a year before the spring of 1943, when mass strikes had made both the people in general and part of the civil service more inclined to resist the Germans. And finally, the Netherlands were particularly isolated; there was no neutral Sweden on the horizon, and, even if there had been, it would have been impossible to carry over a hundred thousand people to safety.

The Danish Jews who were saved, totaled only six thousand.

Despite all this, the Germans did not fully realize their aim. About three thousand Jews managed to escape, either to Belgium and France where they stayed, or to Switzerland and Spain, and about twenty-five thousand went into hiding, about sixteen thousand of whom were not detected. So it may be true that over a hundred thousand Jews were deported, but it is equally true that the Dutch underground tried to save twenty-five thousand Jews. I would like to add that many Jews, my own parents among them, refused the help that was offered them because they believed that deportation gave them a better chance to survive than going into hiding.

I now come to Seyss-Inquart's fourth aim: to prevent any help to Germany's enemies—the Allied powers and the Soviet Union—by espionage, by sabotage, or by guerrilla activity, for instance. I say "for instance" because espionage, sabotage, and guerrilla activity are simply examples. It was the underground that tried to save the twenty-five thousand Jews I have mentioned. And when I pointed out earlier that at the end of the war no fewer than three hundred thousand non-Jewish Dutchmen whom the Germans wanted to use as slave labor in Germany were hiding in the Netherlands, it must be understood that this striking achievement was only possible because they, the *onderduikers,* "underdivers," as they were called, had been given hiding places and often also false identity papers and some money by underground organizations. The largest of these, built up in the course of 1943, eventually comprised no fewer than thirteen thousand underground workers. Starting with the summer of that year, a sort of underdivers-exchange was held every week. It was often camouflaged as a group meeting to discuss particular passages from the Bible. Here the representative of Amsterdam might produce a list of people who wanted to go into hiding, and the representatives of agricultural provinces produced their lists showing the addresses of new hiding places they had found since the last meeting. The information was exchanged, with the result that the volunteers from Amsterdam were provided with addresses to which they could travel and be safe.

This large organization was linked to three smaller ones that had specific tasks. One of them systematically collected information about police measures (whenever the German or the Dutch Nazi police intended to comb through a certain district, it was vitally important to warn those in hiding in time) and information on traitors and other pro-German spies who had to be liquidated. The second smaller organization specialized in faking all the official documents and stamps that had to be used by the underground workers themselves or by those they cared for. The third organization carried out hundreds of raids on population registers, food offices, labor offices, police stations, and sometimes also on prisons. The police stations came first: there, in 1943, the men of this third group had to capture their first hand weapons—Dutch weapons, not British ones.

I have already referred to the fact that the Netherlands were particularly isolated. In order, however, to understand why in the fourth year of the occupation no British arms were available to one of the most important and effective underground groups, three other factors must be mentioned.

First, no preparations had been made by the prewar government to facilitate secret contacts in the event that the country would be occupied. The government believed that it would be able to withstand any German attack for at least a few weeks, if not months, leaving it time to prepare such secret contacts. In fact the campaign lasted only five days, and when the government arrived in London not a single wireless transmitter had been left behind. Both the Netherlands Secret Service and British Military Intelligence and SOE had to start from scratch.

Second, the Netherlands were not of particular military significance to the Allies. In view of the range of most fighter aircraft and the nature of the terrain—sand dunes that were easily defended, broad tracts of land that could be inundated within a few days—it must have been immediately obvious to Allied planners that a large-scale landing on the Dutch coast was out of the question. Aid to the French underground therefore seemed far more important than aid to the Dutch.

Third, although in 1940 and 1941 Dutch Intelligence with the help of British Military Intelligence was able to send its first secret agents into the occupied Netherlands, British SOE made a slow start. Worse yet, early in 1942 the German Secret Services led SOE to believe that some of its wireless operators who had fallen into German hands, were still at liberty. The result of further catastrophic blunders on the part of the British officers concerned was that all operations conducted by SOE from March 1942 to December 1943 were nullified, with heavy losses of life and equipment. Dozens of agents who parachuted into the occupied country fell into German hands, as did all their weapons and explosives. British Military Intelligence too was affected by this notorious so-called *Englandspiel*, and from August 1942 until March 1943, six vital months in the middle of the war, not a single intelligence agent was at liberty in the Netherlands and not one transmitter at work.

Fortunately by that time underground groups in the Netherlands had been able to build up regular courier lines to Sweden and Switzerland, from which countries a constant flow of secret information as well as issues of underground papers were passed on to London.

Early in 1943 the Dutch Intelligence Service in London

was reorganized, and one year later SOE made a new start. By that time several nationwide espionage groups were at work. Some had been set up by secret agents, some by Dutch underground workers. Assisted by London, they constantly expanded their activities. One might say that during the last year of the war at least ten secret transmitters were at work at the same time, and there was not a single German machine-gun nest in the country that had not been reported to Allied Headquarters. Moreover, starting in August 1944, more than two months after D-day in Normandy, SOE was able to drop some 30,000 hand weapons into the country, where they were hidden. Half of the storage places were detected by the Germans, but the remaining weapons enabled the Dutch Forces of the Interior, as they were then called, to provide substantial help to the liberating armies in the eastern and northern parts of the country. In the western part there was no fighting; here the Germans capitulated on May 5, 1945.

I have not yet finished.

Mention must be made of the fact that the Netherlands underground press, which started in the summer of 1940 with a few bulletins of which only mimeographed or even handwritten copies were made, by the end comprised hundreds of papers, the more important of which were printed at regular intervals in tens of thousands of copies, all of which were secretly distributed. In the summer of 1943 the Germans paid a telling compliment to the London broadcasts: all radio sets were confiscated. There were at that time about one million of the sets in the country; my estimate is that about four hundred thousand were kept behind. Most of these, however, could no longer be used during the last phase of the war, for there was no electricity. But the underground press saw to it that daily bulletins on the development of the war were distributed at least in all cities. I give you two figures: the Netherlands State Institute for War Documentation is in possession of more than seventy thousand different issues of over twelve hundred different underground papers, and even this vast collection is not complete.

I have to add that Dutch underground groups saw to it that some three thousand Allied officers and men (prisoners-of-war who had escaped from German camps, and members of the Air Forces who had bailed out or made forced landings) were enabled to pass from the Netherlands via overland routes to Spain whence they could rejoin their units.

Finally, the underground movement in the Netherlands was unique insofar as it numbered one secret organization whose sole task was to collect the money needed to keep all other groups in action and to provide financial support to many of the hundreds of thousands in hiding. For instance, the more than thirty thousand railway workers who had gone on strike in September 1944, after some time all received their weekly wages and even their Christmas bo-

nuses. Think of the effort it took, first to get all that money available and next to have it distributed in small packages in the occupied provinces north of the big rivers. (In that part of the Netherlands about twenty thousand people starved to death during that last wartime winter.) The total expenses of this financial organization alone amounted to over one hundred million guilders (present value: perhaps five hundred million dollars), and when liberation came, all expenses were accounted for, not a single dime having been misappropriated, and all the people and companies from whom money had been borrowed were repaid by the government. The very complexity of Dutch society made it impossible for the Germans to trace this group, which may be called "the banker of Dutch resistance." Its operations are a telling example of the way in which underground groups managed to operate within the folds, so to speak, of a society which the Germans claimed to dominate.

These underground groups suffered heavy losses. There was no postwar registration of all who had taken part in their operations. My estimate is that they totaled some fifty to sixty thousand people, but it should be kept in mind that this estimate does not include all those who gave them assistance, or, for instance, the members of the hundreds of thousands of families that sheltered people whom the Germans wanted to arrest. Of these fifty to sixty thousand underground workers, more than ten thousand

were either shot by the Germans or died in concentration camps. Thousands more were so worn out that they were unable to rebuild their lives after the war ended. And there are other thousands who, although they did rebuild their lives, still suffer from severe depression or from the ordeal of nightmares, all testifying to the tremendous tensions they had to withstand in the months or even years in which they knew themselves to be mercilessly hunted by the Gestapo.

Was it worth it?

The men and women concerned hardly ever doubted it. Apart from that, they simply did what they felt compelled to do. Their religious or political conviction may have played some part in this, but whether or not to join the underground movement (and some people never found the right connections to do so) was primarily a matter of personality, one might say of character. True, some underground workers were mere adventurers, but most were ordinary human beings, living, however, in an extraordinary period of Dutch history. They realized that the reports on their activities acted as a spur to Allied leaders and to public opinion in Allied countries. They also realized that they were fighting an evil power that constituted a threat to civilization and that they were saving countless human lives. True, sometimes there were heated discussions among the leaders of the underground groups, particularly with regard to the question of how the country should be

reorganized and governed after the war; but the internecine fights that were part of the underground struggle in Poland, Yugoslavia, and Greece, and to a limited extent in France, did not occur in the Netherlands. The Dutch underground was in the Dutch tradition: it shunned excesses, it was moderate.

In many ways it still acts as an inspiring element in present-day Dutch society. This is one of the reasons why its historical importance should not be underrated. But it would be equally wrong to make it the subject of romantic adulation. I have tried to present a sober picture.

To sum up. The Germans succeeded by and large in exploiting the economic potential of the Netherlands, and they succeeded in deporting most of the country's Jews. Their attempt at Nazification, however, failed miserably, and they were totally unable to prevent the growth of a flourishing underground movement, whose three main achievements were to keep up people's morale (principally through the underground press); to care for some hundreds of thousands of people who were living in hiding; and to provide the Allies with vital military information.

In 1944 Queen Wilhelmina, who completely identified herself with the men and women of the Dutch underground, in some of her broadcast speeches characterized the Dutch nation as "a nation of heroes." Not a single underground paper felt compelled to approve this qualification. They knew better. Most people, however anti-German their feelings, tried to protect themselves, their families, and their property, adapting themselves to the increasingly difficult circumstances of daily life. It was but a minority that proved willing to accept great personal risks and to put everything, even life itself, at stake.

Nations of heroes do not exist. But there were among the Dutch tens of thousands of ordinary human beings, men and women, who did save the country's soul.

# The Queen's
# "Finest Hour"

As the Holocaust was the central event in the life of every European Jew who is one of the survivors, so the Second World War was the central event in the life of Wilhelmina, Queen of the Netherlands.

In May 1940, when her country was suddenly attacked by Nazi Germany, the Queen, born in August 1880, was in the sixtieth year of her life. Though nearing the threshold of old age (fifty years ago people aged quicker than they do nowadays), she was still vigorous and undaunted. In high government circles in the Netherlands she was one of the very few who had clearly foreseen the German invasion, but the Dutch Constitution allowed her little influence on government policy. The country's real rulers were the leaders of the political parties that were in power. A coalition was usually formed by some of these parties, which together held a majority in parliament, and, if the cabinet ministers acted in agreement with this majority, they could insist that the Queen, whatever her private views, put her signature on all state papers that required it. They, the ministers, were responsible to parliament and public opinion—the Queen, "inviolate" according to one of the most important articles of the Dutch Constitution—was but a shadowy figure in the background. Was she satisfied with this arrangement? By no means. But she was powerless to change it. Moreover, in ascending to the throne in 1898 as an eighteen-year-old girl, she had sworn that she would always act in accordance with the Constitution.

During the days of the German invasion this proved to be far from easy. The Queen was profoundly convinced that she, not the current cabinet, was the true embodiment of the Kingdom of the Netherlands. She was equally convinced that the fate of that Kingdom was inextricably linked with the fate of the age-old House of Orange, whose founder, William the Silent, in the sixteenth century had been the leader during the first phase of the national struggle against Spain which led to the emergence of the Netherlands as an independent power. Queen Wilhelmina abhorred national socialism. It was unthinkable to her ever to be put in a position where she would have to bow to the demands of that brutal upstart Adolf Hitler. Even before the German armies attacked, in the early morning of Friday, May 10, 1940, she had decided that the moment that attack came, Crown Princess Juliana would have to be sent to safety, together with the Princess' husband, Prince Bernhard, and her two infant daughters (the elder of whom, Beatrix, now is Queen of the Netherlands), and that she herself would leave The Hague (the city where she lived and which housed the government departments), as soon as it appeared that she might fall into German hands. In that case she intended to go to the most southwestern part of the country, where French help might be expected. This was exactly what the King of Belgium had done in the early period of the First World War, when his country was overrun by the German armies. And those armies had been unable to conquer the southwestern part of Belgium.

Indeed, Hitler's intention was to capture both Queen Wilhelmina and her cabinet ministers. The airborne troops, however, which landed on the three airfields surrounding The Hague for this purpose, were beaten back, and the Queen and her ministers gained a respite of a few days. There was some delay in the departure of Princess Juliana, her husband, and her two daughters, but on the evening of Sunday, May 12, they were able to board a British destroyer. On Monday morning, when the Germans had broken through the main defense line guarding the western provinces, the Commander-in-Chief of the Dutch armed forces had to inform the Queen that he could no longer guarantee her personal safety. She left immediately. Unhesitatingly? No. She realized that the news of her departure would be a tremendous blow to public opinion and to the morale of the armed forces which continued to resist the Germans. But she consoled herself with the thought that in the southwestern part of the country she would at least remain on Dutch soil. However, the commander of the British destroyer she boarded at The Hook of Holland, the North Sea harbor just west of Rotterdam, had to inform her that the sea route to that southwestern part was too dangerous and that he saw no other solution but to carry her to Britain. She accepted his advice, in tears.

Although the Queen had acted promptly, though not without some doubt whether the course she was following was the right one, on that Monday morning of May 13 the cabinet ministers found it agonizingly difficult to make up their minds. Their cabinet had been formed in August 1939, just before the outbreak of the Second World War. It was a coalition of five of the six most important political parties, one of the five being the socialist party, which never before had been admitted to a cabinet. This party represented nearly a quarter of the electorate, and the Queen had strongly advised the political leader who formed that cabinet, to include the socialists. That leader was a nearly seventy-year-old statesman, Dirk Jan de Geer, a stubborn and wily politician and a man of strong pacifist leanings. He became Prime Minister and minister of Finance. In the 1920s and early 1930s he had put all his trust in the League of Nations; he too abhorred national socialism, but he had clung to the belief that the Netherlands would be able to remain neutral in the Second World War as they had done in the First. On May 10, 1940, all his illusions had shattered, and on the morning of Monday, May 13, he was so nervous that he could hardly dial a telephone, let alone lead the cabinet discussions. Queen Wilhelmina had acted on her own, and the cabinet did not even know that she had left The Hague. Two of the eleven cabinet members—the ministers of Foreign Affairs and of the Colonies—had flown to London on

May 10 in order to speed up British and French assistance. Among the remaining nine ministers, a few now strongly urged that the entire cabinet should immediately try to reach Britain. One of them was the minister of Justice, Pieter Sjoerds Gerbrandy, a sturdy Calvinist who had accepted a seat in the de Geer cabinet contrary to the wishes of the leaders of the Calvinist Party of which he was a member. In the early afternoon six ministers, de Geer among them, followed Gerbrandy's advice and left for The Hook. A few hours later they were joined there by their two colleagues who had originally remained in The Hague. So it was that, again a British destroyer having taken the party on board, early in the morning of Tuesday, May 14, all members of the de Geer cabinet and Queen Wilhelmina found themselves on British soil. In the mind of the Queen there was not a shred of doubt that, whatever the outcome of the fighting in the Netherlands proper, the Kingdom of the Netherlands should continue the struggle. But when, early Tuesday evening, news came through that the Dutch armed forces had capitulated (except in the southwestern part of the country, where resistance was continued for a few days), the cabinet ministers could not reach agreement on a clear and unequivocal statement.

In the weeks that followed the gap between the conviction of the Queen and that of most of the cabinet ministers widened. The Belgian army laid down its arms; the British

Expeditionary Force was evacuated from Dunkirk; France crumbled; and it was widely expected, also by most observers in the United States (though, fortunately, not by President Franklin D. Roosevelt), that the German *Wehrmacht* would soon land on British soil. Queen Wilhelmina's decisions were clear. Crown Princess Juliana and her two daughters were sent to Canada, so that, whatever happened on the British Isles, the dynasty was safe. In case of a German invasion the Queen also would try to cross the Atlantic; but, should that prove impossible, she ordered her private secretary to shoot her. Her fighting spirit manifested itself most clearly in the address with which she inaugurated the daily program of *Radio Oranje*, which was broadcast over the BBC stations. In that address she characterized the war as a struggle between the forces of good and evil, in other words: no compromise with Hitler and his gang of fellow criminals!

Prime Minister de Geer thought differently. The war, as he saw it, was lost; in his opinion the Dutch government had no choice but to approach the German Führer in order to see whether a compromise peace could be obtained. He found no clear support among the members of his cabinet, though most of the ministers did entertain grave doubts whether it was wise to stay in Britain where, they believed, heavy bombing if not heavy fighting would occur. They saw to it that a Dutch seagoing vessel was reserved for their eventual evacuation, and they decided, with Gerbrandy and a few others dissenting, that the seat of the government should be moved to Batavia (now Djakarta), at that time the capital of the Netherlands' most precious colonial possession, the Netherlands Indies. This meant of course that the Queen too would have to go to the Indies. This plan she rejected, choosing an argument which lay outside the political sphere: her health, she said, made it impossible for her to live in a tropical climate.

In taking this stand she acted in close concert with Gerbrandy, and it was again in accordance with his opinion that in August she informed de Geer that she had lost all confidence in him. If at that critical moment he had adopted the position that the Queen's opinion was of no importance to him because his prime ministership had been approved by parliament, a most unhappy situation would have developed. But instead de Geer offered his resignation as prime minister, expecting that he could stay on as minister of Finance. There was only one member of the cabinet in whom the Queen saw the qualities of a fighting leader: Gerbrandy. He accepted her proposal to succeed de Geer, and he rejected the proposal of his colleagues that de Geer should stay on as minister of Finance. The upshot was that de Geer was dismissed both as prime minister and as minister of Finance, and that Gerbrandy, retaining all other members of the de Geer cabinet (they, after all, represented most of the Dutch political parties), assumed the leading position that he would keep until the end of the war, nearly five years later—five long years.

It is difficult enough to describe historical events as they really occurred, and it is no doubt extremely risky to introduce the conception of "if." Sometimes, however, this experiment is too attractive not to be undertaken. The least one can say is this: If Queen Wilhelmina had remained passive, an increasingly wide gulf would have separated the Dutch cabinet in London from major parts of public opinion in the occupied Netherlands, in the Netherlands Indies, and the West Indies; from public opinion among the Dutch in Great Britain; and from the governments of Great Britain, the Commonwealth countries, and the United States. Great damage would have been done to the reputation of the Netherlands; they would, for some time at least, have been equated to Vichy France. Nothing of the sort happened. The discussions between the Queen and most of her ministers never really penetrated to the outside world (although they were known to the British Government), so full Dutch partnership in the momentous struggle that was being waged was never questioned. Political responsibility for the change of government was accepted by Gerbrandy in forming his new cabinet. It is, however, quite clear that historical responsibility lies with no one other than Queen Wilhelmina.

I have described these 1940 events in some detail because they include two initiatives taken by the Queen that clearly have been of historical importance: her decision not to allow herself to become Hitler's prisoner (she did not compromise her position as did King Leopold, who remained in Belgium); and her decision to get rid of de Geer and have him replaced by Gerbrandy. At the same time, however, these events throw light on her valiant personality, and they permit the conclusion that in London, in exile, she had more freedom to act than in the Netherlands. Why? Because there was no parliament. Since her accession to the throne there had been many struggles between the Queen and her ministers, either with individual ministers or with cabinets as a whole. But, as I have pointed out already, whenever a minister or a cabinet said that, in view of the reactions to be expected from parliament, he or they declined responsibility for a line of action proposed by the Queen, the struggle was over and the Queen had lost. It would go too far to describe her in 1940 as an embittered woman, but without a doubt she was deeply frustrated.

These frustrations had their origin in nineteenth-century history.

After Napoleonic times Queen Wilhelmina's great-grandfather King William I was the country's real ruler; the ministers were but his servants. In 1848, however, her grandfather William II bowed to the storms of political revolution in France, Austria, and Germany. Turning, as he said, in one night from conservatism to liberalism, he agreed that the Dutch Constitution should be rewritten in accordance with the unwritten British one. From 1848 on the Dutch executive consisted of two branches that had to present a united front toward parliament and public opinion: the king's inviolability was guaranteed by the fact that political responsibility rested with the ministers. The king having lost most of his power, in 1849, when William II died, the crown prince ascended the throne as King William III without a shred of enthusiasm. In fact he seriously considered refusing to do so.

Now, in Britain, as Walter Bagehot, founder of *The Economist,* was the first to point out, the cabinet being responsible, three rights were retained by the king or queen: the right to encourage; the right to warn; and the right to be informed. It is clear that this third right was the most important one: encouragement as well as warnings should be based on adequate information. At first William III did receive this information, the director of his private office participating in all sessions of the cabinet and even writing the minutes. But in the early 1860s relations between the King and his ministers became so strained that, first, the director of his private office was no longer admitted to cabinet sessions, and, second, the minutes shriveled up to a brief list of some of the decisions taken. While preparing my history of the Netherlands in the Second World War, I was permitted access to the cabinet's minutes for the interwar period. I approached this source with high hopes, but what I found were mainly lists with the names of people who would be proposed to the Queen to be awarded high decorations. Those so-called minutes, which contained no reports on all discussions concerning really important political questions, were sent once a month to the Queen's private office. Of course, she obtained more information. All important state papers were submitted to her, and she would frequently summon the prime minister or individual ministers to give her additional information. However, the distrust between the sovereign and the political leaders that had originated in the nineteenth century remained so strong that, though she might be informed, she was only rarely really consulted.

There was only one period in which relations between Queen Wilhelmina and the prime minister were cordial. That was during the First World War, when the prime minister, a former university professor who had learned to value the Queen's political insight, used to consult her at every critical moment when the country's neutral position seemed to be in danger. In Queen Wilhelmina's personal memoirs, written and published after her abdication, he is the only one of all the ministers who held office during her long reign, who is mentioned with anything close to affection. Almost all the others remain anonymous, "thrown," as she used to say, "in the dustbin of history." Frustration had made her fond of cutting expressions.

I have mentioned some of the reasons for this frustration. There are more.

Although in practice the Queen had little influence, the

customs of the time demanded that she be treated as an all-powerful monarch. No one was allowed to speak to her first, let alone to put questions to her. She was, moreover, assumed never to be in the wrong. Once, as a young woman, she officially visited a textile exhibition where she mentioned to an exhibitor that one of the dresses shown seemed to be made of particularly fine wool. "I am sorry, Your Majesty," the man answered, "it is made of cotton." The Queen having passed on, the man was severely reprimanded. He was told that he should have replied: "Indeed, Your Majesty, this dress is of a sort of wool we happen to call cotton." Multiply an event like this one, try to imagine a situation in which you are constantly the object of veneration and flattery, and you get some idea of the malforming influences exerted on the mind of an ordinary human being who happens to be a king or a queen.

Not the least of these influences is, or at least was, that most people, approaching such an august monarch, lost their natural candor. Queen Wilhelmina who, as I pointed out earlier, saw herself as the embodiment of the state of the Netherlands, was actually treated by many people as if she was that embodiment. Not by all! Socialists and Communists tended to see the Dutch monarchy as a typical symbol of the Dutch bourgeois state, of Dutch capitalism. Even in the 1930s that was the view held by over a quarter of the Dutch electorate. As to the remaining three-quarters, one might say that the Queen was esteemed by

went too far) that after the war, as parts of the Kingdom of the Netherlands, the Netherlands Indies and the West Indies would be put on an equal footing with the mother country in Europe. All other speeches, however, were her own work, and what she said to the occupied nation decisively changed public opinion in her favor. Her voice was clear and vigorous, her words testified to her unbroken spirit. Each of her speeches contained an appeal to resist the foreign invader, valiantly but prudently. The fact that her mother, her husband (who had died in 1934), and her son-in-law were of German descent did not stop her from contemptuously referring to the Germans as *de Moffen*, "the Huns." "Beat them on their head," she said on one occasion. People's deep hatred of the foreign occupier and especially the fighting spirit of all who resisted him or who had joined one of the underground groups were reflected in every speech the Queen made. She also found exactly the right words of compassion for all who suffered persecution. Now, for the first time, to the people at large she was not merely the Queen but at the same time a motherly woman, deeply disturbed by the indignities inflicted upon her children and unshakably convinced that liberation would come and that justice would be meted out to all German war criminals and to those Dutchmen—she called them "scoundrels"—who had traitorously allied themselves with the Third Reich.

For the time being, war and occupation greatly diminished the strength of prewar political antagonisms. There was but one overriding issue: to regain independence. The House of Orange became the symbol of this issue. Those who had been lukewarm about the monarchy or who had even opposed it, changed their feelings and consequently their opinions. One might say that at last virtually the entire nation accepted Queen Wilhelmina as their Queen. As Simon Schama wrote in his study of Dutch culture in the Golden Age, *The Embarrassment of Riches*, nearly three centuries earlier, in 1672, when the Dutch Republic was assailed by Britain, France, and the bishops of Münster and Cologne in Germany, the Stadholder William III became "the living incarnation of the national will." So now Queen Wilhelmina. This she felt and this she knew; she knew it from reports that had been passed along through secret channels and from what she was told by those who succeeded in leaving the occupied Netherlands and reaching London, each of whom was received by her in private audience.

The Queen had always longed to escape from her "golden cage"; what she most deeply wanted was to be accepted as a human being. At the same time, she wanted to be in a position where the main lines of national policy would be determined by her, by the Queen—a position perhaps best compared with that of the president of France. She believed that during the occupation and as a result of it most prewar political dissensions in the Netherlands had lost their importance and their force, and that therefore most prewar political parties would not return, that the people would be much more united, and that in the period of fluidity that would occur after liberation an overwhelming majority would be willing to accept her ideas for the future. These she used to express in one word: *vernieuwing*, "renewal." The Constitution too would have to be changed. She hoped that the first postwar cabinet would be willing to allow her a fairly dominant position and that all changes in the Constitution she considered necessary would be accepted by the first postwar parliament, whose members would be nominated, not elected. In such a parliament, she hoped, the resistance movement and the underground groups would be the strongest force and a united force.

Queen Wilhelmina set about to prepare for this. She refused to sign any of the draft royal decrees of the Gerbrandy cabinet that set forth how that first postwar parliament might best be formed. She also tried to have her son-in-law, Prince Bernhard, appointed Commander-in-Chief of all the Dutch armed forces. That position would be of special importance, because as Commander-in-Chief he would head the Dutch Military Administration, which, immediately after liberation, would virtually run the country under the authority of General Eisenhower, the Supreme Allied Commander, and also because she was confident that Prince Bernhard would always act in her spirit.

All those plans came to naught.

First, General Eisenhower refused to accept a Dutch Commander-in-Chief. A Dutch general was named head of the Military Administration, and Prince Bernhard, in September 1944, had to be content with the position of Commander of the Dutch armed forces, which meant in practice that he controlled the so-called Dutch Forces of the Interior in the liberated provinces south of the big rivers. North of those rivers his control was not very effective.

Second, politically the Dutch underground groups were by no means united as regards the postwar period. Some of the most important ones were of the opinion that the underground movement should not assume a postwar political role. At the end of September 1944 the Queen sent a secret message to the underground movement (a message that was unknown to the Gerbrandy cabinet) in which she invited that movement to send a delegation to London in order to discuss postwar political arrangements. This message merely led to endless debates among the leaders of the underground groups; the outcome was that no delegation was sent.

Third, most of the leaders of the prewar political parties were confident that the Queen was mistaken in her belief that their parties, returning to the scene, would be rejected by public opinion. They foresaw, moreover, that, if there was any change in the power alignment between the Queen and the cabinet, the Queen would be put in a vulnerable position that would endanger both the stability of the country and the future of the House of Orange. In 1942 the Queen and Prime Minister Gerbrandy had been able to get in touch through Switzerland with the leaders of the prewar parties who were meeting in secret from time to time. One of the questions put to them was: Do the people desire a change in the constitutional position of the Queen? They had answered: No. This answer had not deterred the Queen from cherishing the hopes I have indicated, but when liberation came, she realized that for the moment her ideas had found but little support. In the second half of May 1945, after the collapse of Germany, she consulted a wide range of political leaders, leaders of underground groups, and other prominent representatives of the resistance movement in order to determine who would be charged by her to form the first postwar cabinet. None of the people she consulted was asked whether a change was desired in her constitutional position. Indeed no change was effected. The first postwar parliament was mainly a continuation of the last prewar one, which had been elected in 1937. When, in May 1946, general elections took place, all prewar parties (except of course the national socialist party) returned to parliament in more or less their former strength.

That one desire of Queen Wilhelmina—to be accepted by virtually the entire nation—had been fulfilled. It was no small achievement. I do not think any stadholder in the time of the Dutch republic or any monarch of the Kingdom of the Netherlands ever rejoiced in the general affection that Queen Wilhelmina had won. She had greatly strengthened the position of the House of Orange. Nevertheless, her former constitutional position was continued. No less, no more. She had had to give up all hope that that position would be decisively changed in her favor. She reigned, but the Netherlands were governed, as before, by the leaders of the political parties. This was a disappointment. Another disappointment was that the renewal she had dreamt of did not materialize. In this respect the first postwar cabinets, she felt, were too passive, and it hurt her deeply that many authorities who in her opinion had failed during the occupation were maintained in their positions and that those who had risked their life in the underground struggle were but poorly rewarded.

In 1948 Queen Wilhelmina decided to abdicate. It often has been thought that her main reason for doing so was that she foresaw that the Indonesian Republic, proclaimed a few days after Japan's capitulation, was going to win the struggle in the Netherlands Indies, and that she did not wish to enter history as the queen during whose reign that jewel of the Crown was lost. This belief is ill-founded. In 1948 the Queen was still confident that the Dutch armed forces would ensure that the Netherlands would retain much of their influence in the Indonesian Archipelago. The main reason for her abdication was that she felt tired, as well she might. After the Communist coup in Prague in February 1948, and while tension mounted around West Berlin, there were fears that a Third World War might break out. Reflecting on her own attitude in 1940, she came to the conclusion that it would be best for the country to have a queen of youthful strength. "I have lost that strength," she told her private secretary, "and I am terribly afraid that I will commit the blunders of old age."

Early in September 1948 she was succeeded by Juliana, who was presented, so to speak, by her mother to the people of the capital city of Amsterdam with a brief speech, one sentence of which seems to me of special significance. "I am convinced," Wilhelmina said to the new Queen, "that you will know how to lead with a firm and loving hand that one big family which is formed by the people of the Netherlands." It is, I believe, a sentence full of honest misconceptions. Neither the people of the Netherlands nor any other people can ever be considered "one big family," and it would not be, nor could it ever be, Queen Juliana's task to be that people's leader. The sentence is significant because it indicates once again the function Wilhelmina would have loved to exercise, one of real, effective leadership. That function, however, was exclusively hers in that agonizing summer of 1940, and one can only say that every decision she took in what may be called her "finest hour," was the right one and greatly to the benefit of the Netherlands.

As Princess Wilhelmina, she lived in retirement, devoting more and more attention to the ecumenical movement in the churches. In 1959 she published a mainly non-political autobiography under the revealing title: *Lonesome but Not Alone*. Lonesome indeed she had been, but she had always felt herself to be in the company of God, whose guiding hand she believed to discern throughout her whole eventful life. She died at the end of 1962, at the age of eighty-two. When her mortal remains were carried from The Hague to the New Church in Delft, where the burial vault of the House of Orange is, there lay, as she herself had prescribed, only two objects on her casket: a flag of the Netherlands, and the insignia of the country's highest military decoration, awarded to her by her daughter. Only one wreath was affixed to her coffin; on its ribbon were the words: "The united resistance movement of the Netherlands."

Queen Wilhelmina is remembered by the people of my generation with sincere affection. She has, as I see it, two important achievements to her name. In 1940 she saved the country's reputation; and if now, over forty years later, in the Netherlands the monarch is still seen as a healthy and stabilizing element in society, no one made a greater contribution to that view than Queen Wilhelmina. Not because of the changes she at heart desired, but because of the fact that, true to the oath she had sworn as a young girl, she accepted that *no* changes would be effected.

It is one of the most difficult tasks imposed on each of

us by life itself not to pursue dangerous illusions but to accept reality as it is, even if that acceptance is painful. Queen Wilhelmina did. Overcoming her own imperious nature, she gained a victory that assured her a place in Dutch history second to none.